POLYMER CLAY JEWELLERY

Project Book

Learn how to create a
collection of polymer clay jewellery

5 projects inside!

INTRODUCTION

Welcome to the wonderful world of polymer clay jewellery!

This kit has been specifically designed for adults only.

Learning a new skill is always exciting – we're here to help you get started. Polymer clay jewellery making is a fun, experimental way to combine your love of crafting with a love of jewellery. Polymer clay is so versatile - you can create any shape or size with only a rolling pin and a range of cutters. When your design is finished, simply pop them onto a baking tray and place into the oven to heat up and solidify.

As a crafting skill, you can start as simple or as complex as you like. If you prefer, you can use just two colours and a simple circular stencil to stamp out your shapes. Alternatively, you can use a variety of colours, layering these on top of each other and stamping with a stencil. With a little more experience, you can combine two different types of polymer clay techniques by adding both elements to your jewellery finding. You could also use stencils or lace, to create an embossed print effect in your clay.

The smallest piece of clay can go a long way. It's a great way to make multiple pieces of jewellery by using just a small amount of material. Not only can you make multiples of one design, you can then individually personalise these by using different tools and handy bits and bobs around your house to stamp onto your pieces.

This kit provides everything you need to make your first piece of art, which means getting started is easy. We have included four other projects within this book to help you along the way. Just like any new skill, polymer clay crafting may be a little tricky at first. Experiment with different colours and techniques. But most importantly, enjoy yourself.

Let's get started on your polymer clay jewellery journey.

KIT CONTENTS

WHAT'S INCLUDED:

· Polymer clay
· Cutter
· Clay roller
· 4x Head pins
· 4x Jump rings

WHAT YOU'LL NEED:

· Clay roller
· Round nose pliers
· Cocktail stick
· Baking tray
· Baking paper

Optional Extras:
· Stencil
· Range of different shaped cutters
· Different range of coloured polymer clay

Ingredients:
Kaoline, Aluminium oxide, Water, Iron oxide.

ABOUT POLYMER CLAY:

When you first take out your polymer clay, you will notice it may feel very solid and difficult to manipulate. This is because, the longer your clay has been sitting in a block untouched, the harder it can become. It can also harden when cold, so if your clay has been in its packet for a while on a shelf, or left uncovered, it will naturally harden in this time. That being said, your polymer clay holds the qualities of a soft and malleable material.

HOW TO PREPARE POLYMER CLAY:

Before starting any crafting with polymer clay, you must first knead and condition your clay. This is done by hand, and is a necessary part of polymer jewellery making. The more you knead your clay, the softer it becomes. This makes it easier to fully manipulate into the shapes you want to achieve. To knead your clay, push your fingers into the clay, pressing and twisting it - the warmth of your hands will also naturally soften your clay. This process should take you no more than 10 minutes.

BAKING THE CLAY:

Once you have created your clay masterpieces, it will then be time to bake in the oven*, prior to adding any jewellery findings. This is done by lining a baking tray with parchment paper, placing your clay creations on the tray, and inserting this directly into the oven. The baking process isn't a long one, but the time it takes will depend on the type of polymer clay you are using. For example; the clay we have provided will need to be baked at a temperature of 140°c for 15 minutes.

TURNING THE CLAY INTO JEWELLERY:

After your pieces have fully cooled down, you can add your jewellery findings using your round nose pliers, thus creating amazing pieces of jewellery.

*Not suitable for microwave ovens.

MARBLING:

Marbling your clay is one of the most effective, yet simplest techniques you can do with your clay. You can achieve this by using any amount of colours of your choice. Break a little bit of clay off each block and knead them, so they blend together. Once blended, simply roll out the clay with your rolling pin and admire the marbling effect you have created. This technique can also be achieved by using the excess clay you have left over from other designs.

KNOTTING:

Knotting is a little more complicated, but still very achievable with a bit of patience! To form a knot with your clay, roll your clay into a rope like shape - thin enough to be able to twist without breaking. Now, form a loop with one end of your clay. Thread the other end through the loop, gently pulling until your knot has been fully formed in the middle. Finally, snip off the ends of excess clay and smooth them down before baking in the oven.

EMBOSSING:

Embossing clay is the art of printing a design from a stencil onto your clay to create gorgeous stenciled effects. You can use shop bought stencils or things that can be found around the house – a piece of lace is a brilliant object to create an embossed look! Lay your stencil or lace on top of your rolled out clay and gently apply pressure (this is best done using a rolling pin). Now, carefully peel it off to reveal your design underneath!

TOP TIPS:

Before you begin, make sure your hands are washed and dry, and your work surface is clean and dust free. The clay is very soft and at this stage, any little bit of dust or dirt can stick to it. Once baked, this will be quite tricky to get off!

Always knead your clay before starting to mould or shape it. The kneading process is important, as this will soften the clay and help to remove any air bubbles prior to you creating your jewellery pieces.

ADDED EXTRAS:

Below are some other ways you can develop your clay creations using the skills you will learn in this book.

ADDING A THIRD COLOUR:

In our second additional make, we will learn how to create a clay knot necklace using two colours intertwined. It's always a good idea when laying out your clay to add in an additional colour and make an extra duplicate if you can. This enables you to have variation and choice when creating your jewellery. As clay knots are threaded onto the chain, these can be added and removed for different looks and outfits. So, instead of just trying one – why not try all three!?

USING EXCESS CLAY:

Here's another idea for a pair of earrings! Sometimes you will have clay left over. This can be used to make two smaller circular shapes, these can be attached to larger circular shapes using jump rings. You can then add your earring findings to the smaller circular shapes to create a longer earring style.

WARNINGS!

All the makes included in this book are designed specifically for adults.

Keep all ingredients out of the reach of children.

Some ingredients may irritate; always avoid contact with skin and eyes. If ingredients come into contact with eyes or skin, wash with water immediately.

Do not ingest; if accidentally ingested drink water and seek medical advice. Never leave the oven on when unattended, even if you're just popping out for a minute. Use oven gloves or similar when taking objects out of the oven. Always turn off the oven when not in use. Keep children and pets away from hot ovens.

We recommend wearing old clothes or overalls when partaking in creative activities. Cover work surfaces to avoid mess.

MAKE
WITH KIT
CONTENTS!

BLOCK COLOUR &
MARBLE EARRINGS

BLOCK COLOUR & MARBLE EARRINGS

Bring some colour to your life with these beautiful block colour earrings, follow the steps below to create two amazing designs!

YOU WILL NEED

- Baking tray
- Baking paper
- Cocktail stick

KIT CONTENTS

- Polymer clay
- Cutter
- Clay roller
- 4x head pins
- 4x jump rings

METHOD

1. Gather the materials that you are going to need. We are also going to cut off a small piece of clay from each colour which, in step 2, you will use to create your third colour. Knead and condition both your remaining clay blocks. Make sure to wash your hands in-between kneading each colour.

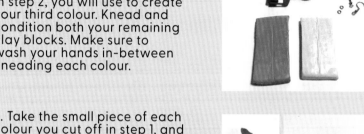

2. Take the small piece of each colour you cut off in step 1, and roll both into a long rope shape. Twist the darker orange rope around your lighter colour and knead together by hand until you have created your third colour. It should resemble a lovely shade of orange when you're finished.

3. You should now have three colours of clay ready to use. Roll each colour into individual rope shapes, about 20cm in length. Lay them out horizontally against each other. Make sure the lightest colour is the last colour to lay at the top. Using your clay roller, roll over all the clay to blend the colours and bind them softly together.

4. Be careful not to roll your clay too thin. As a general rule for earrings, we would say about 2mm thickness is good! Once the clay is flat and smooth, use your knife cutter to cut out the shape you would like. If you have a stencil cutter available, this will make this step a little easier.

5. Pop the excess clay to the side for later. Now, it's time to bake your clay! Before placing the clay in the oven, make small holes in your clay for your jewellery findings to go through easily at the end. This must be done prior to baking! Grab a cocktail stick and slowly push it all the way through the clay, around 2-3mm from the top of your shape. Line a baking tray with baking paper and lay your earrings on the tray. Place in a preheated oven at 140°c for 15 minutes.

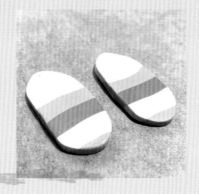

6. Once your earrings have baked, let them cool off until they are cold to touch. Now, you can attach your findings! Firstly, you will need to open your jump rings with a pair of round nose pliers. Hook your fishhook earring onto this. Feed the open jump ring through the hole in the clay and then close it up again with your round nose pliers. Repeat for the second earring. Well done!

METHOD

1. Clean down your work surface with a damp cloth to get rid of any previous clay. Dry thoroughly. Using your hands, roll the clay from your previous cuttings into a rope shape as before.

2. Curl it into a spiral and then knead it using your fingers until you have a semi-flat piece of clay. The colours should have gently marbled together.

3. Gently roll over your clay with your clay roller, making sure to keep a smooth, even surface throughout. Continue until your clay is approximately 2mm thick.

4. Now, you are going to cut your shapes. You can either mirror the shape you cut out before using your knife cutter, or if you are feeling a little bit more confident and you have stencil cutters, you can press your shape into the clay. Leave for 5 seconds and then gently remove your cutter.

5. Repeat this process for the second earring. Following the same method as before, make small holes in your earrings using a cocktail stick. Now, place them onto a piece of baking paper on your baking tray. Pop into a preheated oven at 140°c for 15 minutes.

6. Remove from the oven, and let your clay cool until it is cold to touch. Now, attach your jump ring and fishhook earring the same way you did in your first make. You now have a beautiful pair of marbled polymer clay earrings!

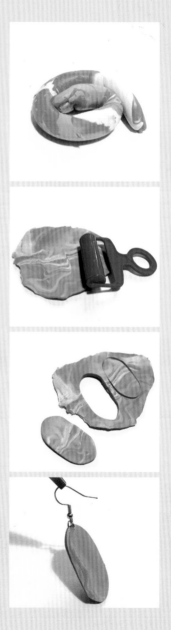

Top Tip – Always use a smooth, hard surface to create your polymer clay pieces on, like a marble kitchen counter or an easy to wipe glass table. Polymer clay can become sticky as it warms. By using a resilient surface like this, it will prevent your clay from sticking to its base. If you do work on a kitchen counter or table, remember to protect it by working on top of a piece of baking paper.

NOTES

Use the space below to make your own personal notes on the previous project to help when you come back to make it again!

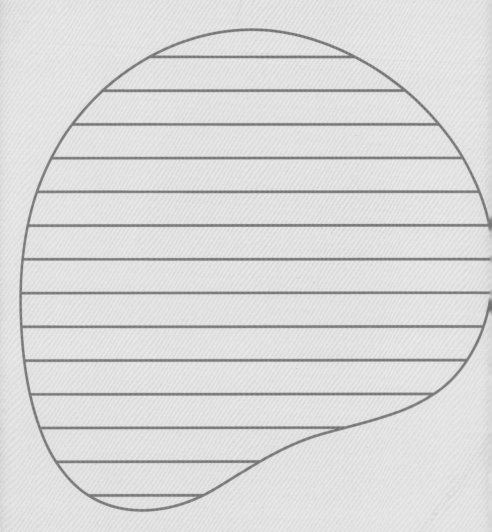

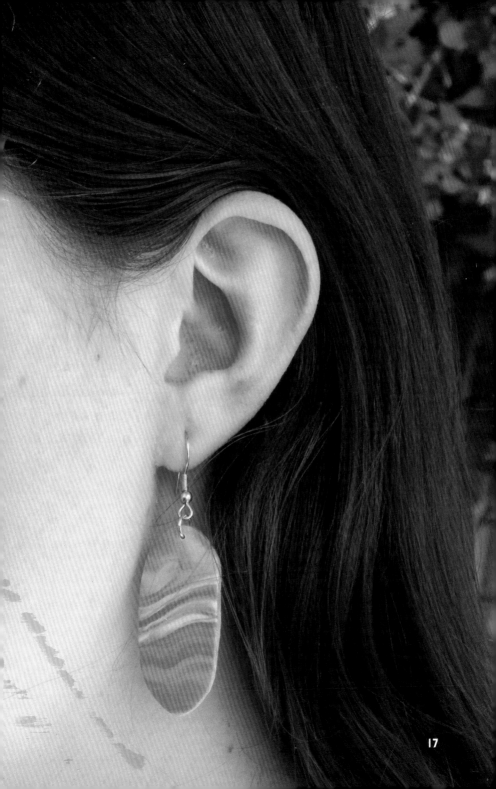

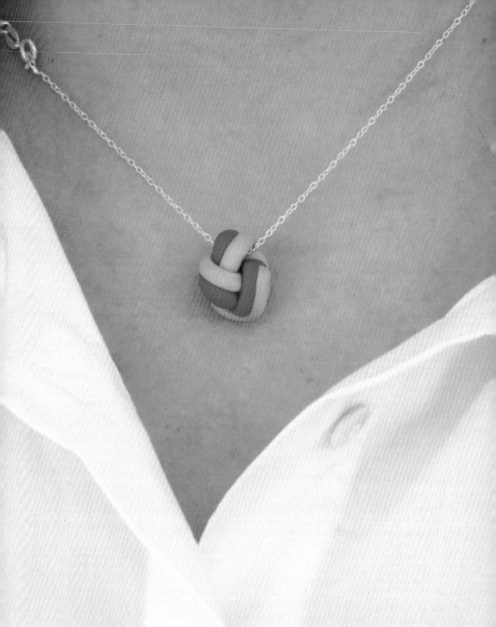

KNOT NECKLACE

KNOT NECKLACE

Using your new skills you've learnt from the first make, why not use them to create this playful necklace for yourself or to gift to a friend?

YOU WILL NEED

· Polymer clay
· Cutter
· Silver chain
· Cocktail stick
· Baking tray
· Baking paper

METHOD

1. Choose any two colours for this make. We are going to show you how to create a knot with your clay using one colour, and then combining two together. Firstly, individually knead both colours of your clay until both are smooth and easy to manipulate.

2. Once your clay is kneaded, roll each colour in the palm of your hands to create that rope shape as before, this time measuring approximately 10cm in length. Take the end of one piece of your clay and loop it over the middle, making sure to pass the opposite end through. Gently pull to tighten the knot. Repeat this with both colours.

3. Once both knots have been created, use your cutting knife to very carefully cut off the excess clay. Leave this clay to one side.

4. Using the excess clay from each colour, re-roll them back into rope shapes. This time, lay them horizontally one on top of the other. Repeat the knotting process in step 2, knotting both colours at the same time.

5. When you have made your two colour knot, cut off the excess as before using your cutting knife. Take a cocktail stick and make sure you can easily fit this through the gap in your knot. This is where your necklace chain will feed through. Do this for all three of your knots.

6. Now pop them in the oven! Once they have been baked and are cool, feed your chain through. Well done! Your new polymer clay knot necklace is ready to wear!

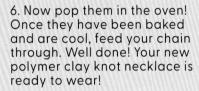

NOTES

Use the space below to make your own personal notes on the previous project to help when you come back to make it again!

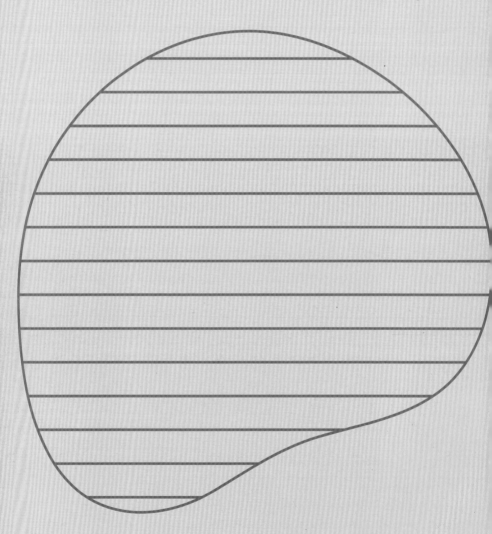

BEAD NECKLACE

BEAD NECKLACE

Create this simple yet stylish necklace using your new skills! Have fun and add your own style to this design by picking different colours of clay to make this necklace.

YOU WILL NEED

- Polymer clay
- Silver chain
- Baking tray
- Baking paper
- Cocktail stick

METHOD

1. This next make is a nice, simple one! Take 4 colours of your choice - make sure you have a little extra as we are going to be breaking a little bit off to make marbled beads! One by one, condition your clay pieces by using the kneading process. Remember to clean your hands in-between each one so the colours do not bleed into the next colour.

2. It's time to make the two marbled beads. Choose a small amount of any other colour, and work it into your white clay by pushing and rolling it with your fingers – this is your third bead. To create your fourth bead, you are going to marble your darkest colour with another one of your choice. For this we have chosen the red and the pink. Take a tiny piece of each colour and knead these together until it has all been mixed in.

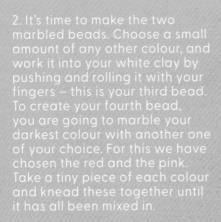

3. One by one, roll each piece of clay into a ball in the palms of your hands, making sure they are roughly the same size.

4. When you have created all 5 of your beads, use your cocktail stick to pierce holes straight through the middle. Make sure the holes are big enough for the chain you have chosen to use.

5. Lay your beads on the baking tray and bake in a preheated oven until hard. (Please refer to the packet instructions of the polymer clay you are using for the appropriate temperature and timings).

6. When the clay has been baked and cooled, remove your beads from the baking tray and feed through your chain – your beads can go in whatever order you wish!

NOTES

Use the space below to make your own personal notes on the previous project to help when you come back to make it again!

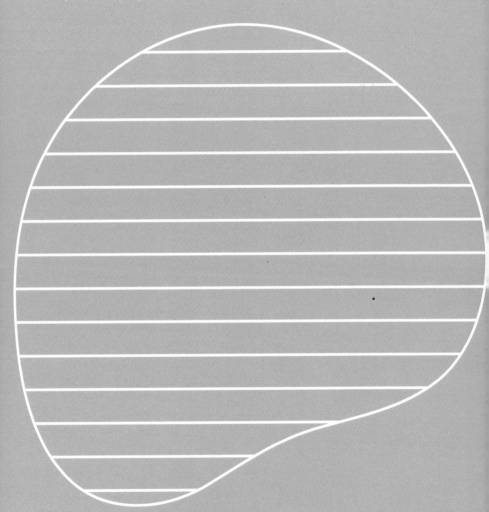

RAINBOW EARRINGS

RAINBOW EARRINGS

Add some colour to your existing jewellery collection with this fun and playful design!

YOU WILL NEED

- Polymer clay
- Cutter
- Clay roller
- Cocktail stick
- Hoop earrings (of your choice)
- Baking tray
- Baking paper

METHOD

1. Take 3 colours of your choice, and lay all your tools out in front of you on a clean, dry work surface. One by one, gently knead and condition each colour of clay until it is soft and elasticated enough to mould. Remove a tiny piece of your blue clay and pop this to the side for Step 5.

2. Using your cutter knife, roughly divide your darkest colour into two pieces. Roll each piece out into long rope shapes approximately 10cm in length. Make one of your blue pieces a little shorter. This will be the middle part of your rainbow.

3. Starting with the shortest piece of blue, fold it over itself, making sure to try and keep the straight parts of the middle vertically aligned. Repeat with the orange over the top, and then again, with your longest piece of blue on top of that one. Pierce the top part of your rainbow with a cocktail stick to create your jewellery incisions as before.

4. Continuing to use your cocktail stick, go around the edges of your rainbow and very gently indent the clay with the sharp point. This will create a nice unique design on your clay.

5. Taking your white clay and the little piece of blue you popped aside in step 1, bind these together using the kneading process. Once blended, roll out with your clay roller until you have a smooth flat surface. Using a circular stencil cutter or your cutting knife, cut out two small circular pieces of clay. Pierce holes as before, using the cocktail stick.

6. Pop all four pieces of clay into the oven and bake for the recommended time on your packet. Once your pieces have completely cooled, feed these through your jewellery findings. Make sure your smaller white disks are sitting comfortably on top of your rainbow designs and can move easily.

NOTES

Use the space below to make your own personal notes on the previous project to help when you come back to make it again!

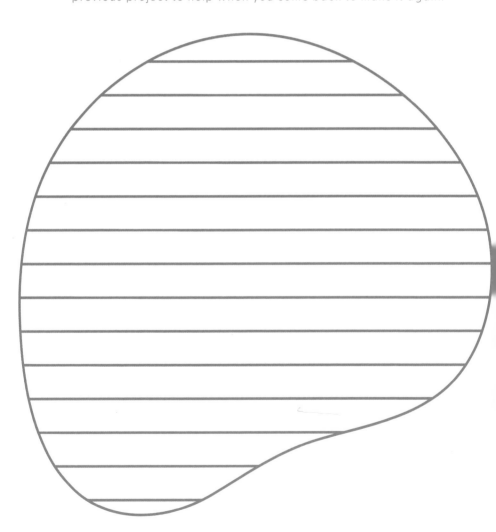

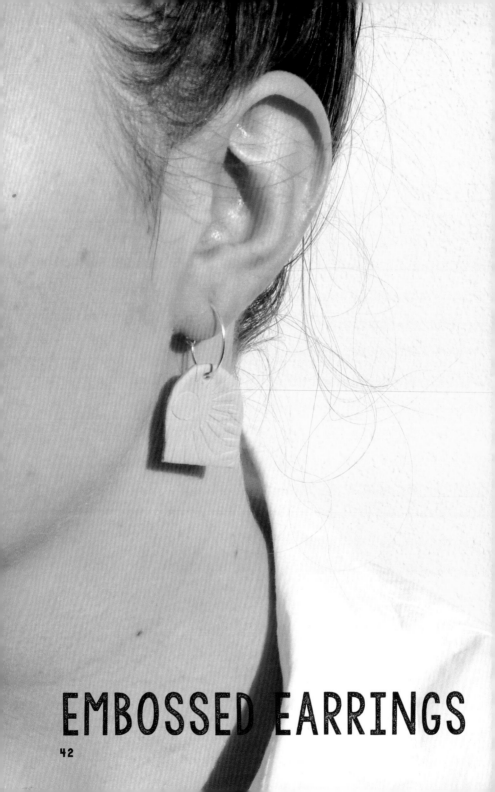

EMBOSSED EARRINGS

EMBOSSED EARRINGS

Now you know the basics of polymer clay, lets step things up a level by embossing some earrings using stencils or lace. You can create these stylish earrings all by yourself.

YOU WILL NEED

- Polymer clay
- Cutter
- Clay roller
- Stencil/ Lace
- Baking tray
- Baking paper
- Cocktail stick

METHOD

1. Now, this is where your polymer clay can get a little bit more exciting! Have a hunt around your house and see if you have any interesting stencils or lace designs you would like to print onto your clay. Gather them together with your other tools.

2. As before, knead and condition your clay by hand until you have the consistency which by now, you should have mastered! Then, lay your stencil down very gently on top of your clay. Be careful not to get any fingerprints on your clay.

3. Holding onto your clay roller tightly, roll over the top of your stencil. Use just enough pressure to make sure the stencil is printing nicely into your clay.

4. Remove your stencil and have a look! If there are still parts of your clay that haven't been printed on, move your stencil around in a circular motion and lay it back down. Keep printing until all of your clay has been covered.

5. Once you are happy with your printed surface, pop your stencil cutter down onto your clay and push down to cut your intended shape. Remove and repeat for your second earring. Once you are happy, make your hole incisions with your cocktail stick & pop into the oven!

6. When the clay has cooled, remove from the baking tray and feed through your jewellery findings. If you want to attach a fishhook earring instead of a hook, this can be done following the process in step 6 of the main make.

NOTES

Use the space below to make your own personal notes on the previous project to help when you come back to make it again!